Attracting Birds

◆

Elaine Butler

© 1991 by Lone Pine Publishing
First Printed in 1991   10   9   8   7   6
Printed in Canada

THE PUBLISHER: Lone Pine Publishing

10145–81 Avenue	1808 B Street NW, Suite 140
Edmonton, AB T6E 1W9	Auburn, WA
Canada	USA 98001

National Library of Canada Cataloguing in Publication Data
Butler, Elaine, 1947-
    Attracting birds

(Home world)
ISBN 0-919433-87-1

1. Birds, Attracting of. 2. Bird feeders.
3. Gardening to attract wildlife—Canada

I. Title. II. Series: Home world (Edmonton, Alta)
QL676.5.B88 1991   639.9'782971   C91-091047-2

Editorial: Phillip Kennedy
Design and Artwork: Beata Kurpinski
Cover Illustration: Horst H. Krause

The publisher gratefully acknowledges the support of Alberta Community Development and the Department of Canadian Heritage.

PC: P9

Contents

Introduction

Attracting birds to back yard feeders is a wonderful way to enjoy the world outside every day of the year.

Watching birds by the window can relieve the boredom of confinement during the long, cold winter, and watching busy parent birds gathering food for their ever-hungry broods adds zest to summer's pleasures. In the midst of the noisy, hectic city, birdwatching can reveal a life beyond office buildings and shopping centres. A refreshing glimpse of wild nature can be as far away as a city park, or as near as the back yard.

Feeding birds is an activity that can be enjoyed throughout one's life. Children can maintain a simple bird feeder by themselves. They don't need to know the names of the birds to enjoy watching them come to the feeder, but with a simple bird guide, they can learn to identify the different species. With a window feeder, even the bedridden can enjoy watching birds.

Putting out food in the winter is also important for the birds, as it increases their chances of surviving the cold nights. When temperatures reach -30 to -40°C, birds start to depend on the fat supplies in their bodies to keep warm through the night. Studies have shown that birds that have access to feeders are fatter and, therefore, better prepared for the cold. Feeders also help individual birds of migrating species which, for some reason, have stayed in the north rather than flying south. They may have trouble finding their usual food supplies which may either be covered by snow or may just not be available at that time of year. A bird feeder can be very important in helping them survive the winter.

There are also practical benefits. When birds are nesting in the summer, they need a lot of insects to feed their young; woodpeckers, nuthatches, and Brown Creepers search trees for borer grubs year-round. If these birds are nesting in the yard, or are coming there to feed, they'll look for insects. In this way birds help to keep the trees, shrubs and flowers healthier. And if Purple Martins or other types of swallows begin to nest in the yard, they will help to control mosquitoes.

Birds can be fed almost anywhere. A single family home with a back yard provides the best opportunity for an elaborate arrangement of feeders and bird-attracting landscaping. Apartment dwellers can still put out window feeders; near parks, ravines or other wooded areas, such feeders attract quite a variety of interesting birds.

Many seniors' lodges and nursing homes have found that bird feeders are a valuable and therapeutic diversion for the residents, particularly during the winter when other activities are more difficult. Bird feeders can be at their most active and interesting in that very season, since the winter finches that use them are willing to come up close for food, where they are easily observed.

Starting With
A Simple Feeder Plan

An elaborate or complicated collection of feeders is not needed to bring birds into the back yard: one or two will do, perhaps a large covered shelf feeder on a pole, a small feeder resting on a table or plank, or a tube feeder hanging from a tree. Add a suet feeder to bring in woodpeckers that wouldn't come to the seed, and to provide a greater variety of food for the chickadees, nuthatches and magpies.

Birds are messy, fussy eaters, and often knock more food off the feeder than they eat. However, since some birds like Morning Doves, juncoes, and White-crowned Sparrows prefer to eat their food off the ground, this creates another feeding area and lessens the competition for food. This

A yard with a simple feeder plan, using one tray and one hopper feeder. This system is good for the casual birder or the person who prefers an open, neatly manicured yard.

doesn't work for sunflower seeds, however. If they fall, they're wasted, since most of the birds that eat them won't feed on the ground.

Feeders for Apartment Dwellers

If there is no back yard, an apartment balcony or a window ledge can be used for setting up a bird feeder. In fact a balcony can be a very successful feeding area. A simple board across the angle of one corner of the balcony railing makes a very good feeding table. Add a suet feeder or a hanging tube of sunflower seeds to increase the variety of birds that will come in. A hopper feeder can also be attached (see *Types of Feeders*) to the board, so that the seed will last longer.

A window feeder can also provide a lot of fun and interest. A platform extending out from the window sill is all that is needed. Add a small railing along the outside edge, and the birds will have a place to land and sit as they feed. A hopper feeder on one end and a suet holder on the other will provide some variety of food. If objects can't be attached to the window sill, there are a number of different feeders made of plexiglass that can be fixed to the window itself with suction cups. These can be found at local nature centres, feed stores, hardware stores, supermarkets and specialty stores. Hopper feeders make a nice addition to a balcony feeder or window sill platform. Fill them with sunflower seeds and watch the chickadees come in.

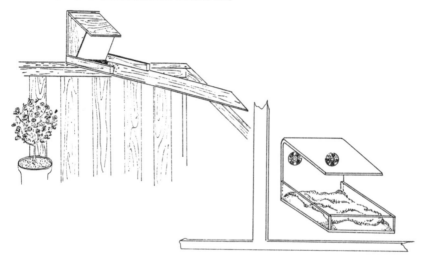

The first visitors are most likely to be House Sparrows, jays, magpies or, in the heart of the city, Rock Doves, but other birds will see their feeding activity and come in to investigate. In an area without many trees or in a very new development, there won't be as many birds as can be found in older, greener neighbourhoods or outside the city. Still, the birds that do come will provide a lot of enjoyment — even if they're only Rock Doves. In a new neighborhood, the chapter on landscaping can be used to plan a yard so that in five to ten years a much richer variety of birds will come.

Getting Birds to Come

It may be more difficult to attract birds with a balcony or window feeder than with a back yard feeder. Normally the first bird may take a day or two to find it. Make it easier for the birds by putting out bread crumbs or crumbled bakery goods—something that the sparrows can easily recognize as food. Birds are naturally attracted to plants as they search for insects and seeds. On a balcony or window sill, try to add some greenery—perhaps a potted shrub or evergreen, or branches from an evergreen fastened around the edges of a feeder platform. Plastic flowers and greenery could also be used. Try sticking some leafy green twigs around plastic feeders that attach to the window.

Setting Up
A Feeder System

A combination of several different types of feeders can be used to attract the greatest variety of birds. Certain birds prefer certain feed dispensers; chickadees will come to just about any feeder but rarely take seeds off the ground, and woodpeckers will come only to suet or peanut butter feeders that are either hanging or attached to the trunk of a tree.

The easiest birds to accommodate are the ground feeders. White-crowned and White-throated Sparrows, American Robins, Ovenbirds and towhees are birds that prefer to search the ground for seeds or insects and worms. To bring the ground feeders that eat seeds to a back yard, scatter food on the ground either below the feeders or under the cover of some evergreens. To attract insect-eating ground feeders like Ovenbirds, see the chapter on landscaping.

Finches like feeders that are off the ground, either up on a post or hanging from a tree or eave. They'll use tray, hopper-style, or hanging tube feeders with perches.

Woodpeckers and nuthatches are used to clinging to tree trunks and branches while looking for the insects and grubs they eat, so they prefer suet or peanut butter feeders that are attached to the side of a tree or post or hanging from a tree branch. Nuthatches are a bit more flexible and will also take sunflower seeds from hanging feeders, but usually they like to retreat to a tree to open and eat them.

Types of Feeders

There is a wide variety of bird feeders available commercially in nature centres, hardware stores, supermarkets, variety stores, specialty bird stores, and mail-order catalogues. Building feeders at home can be especially rewarding; the possible designs are limited only by the imagination. Birds will take food out of a plastic bottle dispenser as readily as from a painted, roofed and gabled feeder with weathervane. On the west coast, cedar rounds sitting on upended logs are often used as feeders.

Feeders can be divided into four general types: trays, hoppers, hangers and suet feeders. The types are sometimes combined.

Tray Feeders

Platform or tray feeders can accommodate a number of birds at one time. When bird feeders are put in a yard for the first time, an open tray feeder will attract birds more quickly than either a covered one or a hopper feeder, because the birds can see the food from a distance more easily. Once birds have started to come, a roof can be added, which will keep the feed from caking or getting wet and moldy. It will also keep the snow off so that the birds can get to the food during and immediately after a snowstorm.

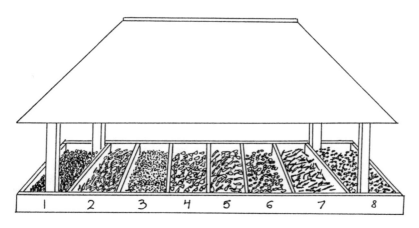

Covered tray feeder with compartments for differend types of seed.

Hopper Feeders

Hopper feeders have a reservoir that can hold from several days' to a few weeks' worth of food, depending upon the size of the feeder and the number of birds using it. Most of them have landing perches and access to the food on at least two sides, increasing the number of birds that can feed at once. Hopper feeders can be hung from a branch (which must be large enough to hold the weight of the feeder securely when it is full of seeds) or from an overhanging eave or beam, or they can be mounted on a post.

Hanging Tubes and Bowls

A number of plastic feeders are commercially available in tube and bowl designs. As they are transparent, it is quite easy to see when the seed is low. Some of them are designed specifically for smaller birds so that Blue Jays don't eat all the sunflower seeds.

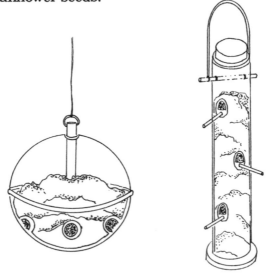

Suet and Peanut Butter Feeders

Perhaps the most common or traditional suet feeder is the plastic mesh onion bag, but there are many different ways to provide suet for the birds, including mass produced latex-covered wire boxes. Suet feeders can also be made out of aluminum food trays or cups, large pine cones, short tin cans, coconut shells and plastic berry boxes. Chicken wire nailed around three sides of a piece of wood with a flap at the top also makes a good holder. Attach the feeders to the side of a tree or hang them from a limb. If there are Pileated Woodpeckers in the neighbourhood, they need at least one feeder on a tree, or a large stable hanging one. They're so big that they have trouble using smaller hanging feeders.

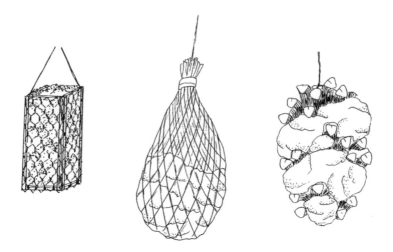

Placement of Feeders

One of the most important points about placing feeders is to have them in sight of a good viewing window. If the birds can't be watched from a comfortable and convenient spot inside, most of the enjoyment which comes from having feeders will be missed.

The feeders need to be placed where they are sheltered from the cold winter winds. If the yard doesn't have any natural windbreaks, such as trees or shrubs, or structures such as a garage or fence, then one can be built into the feeder. It is also important to have a tree, a shrub, or some other structure to provide a landing perch. Birds often prefer to land in a nearby tree or shrub before flying to the feeder, and they also need a place to sit while they're waiting for larger or more aggressive birds to leave.

Some books on attracting birds recommend that feeders be at least nine metres apart from each other, but this isn't necessary; birds like clusters of feeders just as well. Nuthatches in particular like to visit suet boxes, peanut butter feeders and sunflower seed troughs in just one stop. How-

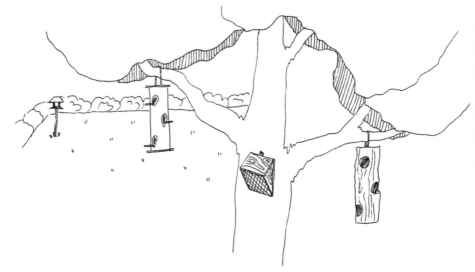

A yard with two feeding areas: one at the pole feeder, a second at the tree with suet and sunflower feeders.

ever, it does help to have another feeder or cluster of feeders farther away. This keeps one or two dominant birds or aggressive flocks from chasing other smaller birds away. It also can be used to segregate types of birds. For example, hanging tubes filled with sunflower or niger seeds can be placed by themselves so chickadees or goldfinches can access them while the sparrows are busy at a tray feeder.

A yard full of feeding birds is very attractive to cats, so it is necessary to take some precautions to protect the birds. The hanging feeders must be at least two metres above the ground, and feeders on posts at least three metres from any other post or fence. Cats usually like to lie in wait before pouncing on a bird; the farther a cat has to run, the better chance the birds have of flying away. Therefore feeding areas should be kept away from ground cover. If that's not possible, put a wire fence around the feeding area or between the cover and the feeding area. That should slow down the cat enough to make it difficult for him to catch a bird.

Bringing Them in Closer

Even if several feeders have been set up in the yard, a window feeder will help bring the birds closer. A window feeder could be a cantilevered ledge or a suction-cup plastic feeder. If it is difficult to get birds to come to the window, it may be because they don't feel any need to come that close, they're afraid to come in, or because they simply don't know the feeders are there. Try putting a special food at the window that isn't available at the other feeders— one that is particularly popular. Or try slowly moving one of the hanging or pole feeders closer and closer to the house until the birds discover the window feeder. Then move it back to its permanent position.

What to Feed
The Birds

Once the feeders are up, they need to be filled with the right foods. The easiest solution is to use the mixed bird seed available at the supermarket; however, commercial mixtures tend to use a lot of red milo seed for bulk, even though very few birds eat it. It's actually more economical to patronize the seed sale at a local nature centre or buy and mix seed from a feed mill.

To make a seed mix, begin with a basic mix primarily made of white proso millet, the most popular small seed. Choose either of the following recipes:

Basic Feed Mixes

A:
45% white proso millet
35% black oil or striped sunflower seeds
20% safflower seeds

B:
55% white proso millet
35% finely cracked corn
10% black oil or striped sunflower seeds

Because of the higher cost of safflower seeds, Mix B will probably be less expensive. Seed can usually be bought in bulk at a local feed mill, often in quantities of 2 to 25 kg. Unusual seeds or mixes may be available at a pet store or feed mill that caters to tropical birds.

While white millet, corn and sunflower seeds are popular with birds everywhere, the same doesn't seem to be true with other seeds; feeding habits vary from region to region. Perhaps it's just a difference of opinion among authors. For example, while most authors agree that sunflower seeds are a staple food, they disagree on which variety is more popular, the black oil (small, black, high oil content) or the striped (large, black or grey with white stripes). Therefore, it's a good idea to test all types of seeds to see which the local birds prefer.

To be systematic about it, use a test tray — an open tray feeder divided into a number of compartments, or even a plastic ice cube tray. Fill each compartment with a different type of seed and see which ones have to be refilled most often. This test can be repeated in the summer, since there will be a different mix of birds at that time. Also, because of the demands of nesting, the birds will have different nutritional needs. Some of the seeds that can be tested are canary seed, safflower, untreated canola, hemp and yellow millet.

In addition to feeding stations carrying the basic mix, separate feeders filled only with sunflower seeds, and a smaller hanging tube or bowl feeder with niger or canola seed should also be provided. Niger seed is particularly prized by goldfinches; both niger and canola seed may also be popular with redpolls and siskins. These special, single seed feeders can form a separate cluster, either by themselves or with the suet. However, if there is only one feeder, it should have a healthy percentage of sunflower seeds in it.

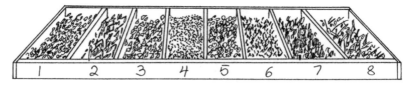

A tray feeder for testing which seeds the birds in your back yard prefer.

Food Preference Chart Small Seeds and Grains

Millet:
House Sparrow, Mourning Dove, White-crowned Sparrow, White-throated Sparrow, Purple Finch, House Finch, redpolls, Pine Siskin, American Goldfinch, Vesper Sparrow, Dark-eyed Junco, Tree Sparrow, Fox Sparrow, Song Sparrow

Oats:
White-throated Sparrow, White-crowned Sparrow, Ruffed Grouse, quail, Mourning Dove, chickadees, Yellow-headed and Red-winged Blackbird, Snow Bunting

Thistle:
American Goldfinch, House Finch, Mourning Dove, Purple Finch, Red- and White-winged Crossbill, Dark-eyed Junco, Common and Hoary Redpoll, Pine Siskin, Song Sparrow, White-throated Sparrow, Brown Thrasher, buntings

Corn:
Blue Jay, Common Grackle, House Sparrow, Mourning Dove, White-crowned Sparrow, White-throated Sparrow, Northern Flicker, Evening Grosbeak, Ruffed and Sharp-tailed Grouse, Steller's Jay, Dark-eyed Junco, White-breasted Nuthatch, Gray Partridge, Ring-necked Pheasant, Common and Hoary Redpoll, American Robin, Fox and Savannah Sparrow, Rufous-sided Towhee, Wild Turkey, ducks, geese

Wheat:
House Finch, House Sparrow, Mourning Dove, White-throated Sparrow, Bohemian Waxwing

Canola:
House Finch, Cassin's Finch, Purple Finch, Common and Hoary Redpoll, American Goldfinch, Pine Siskin, Song Sparrow

Hemp:
Chickadee, White-breasted Nuthatch, Purple and House Finch, redpolls, Pine Siskin, American Goldfinch, Vesper Sparrow, Dark-eyed Juncoe, White-crowned and White-throated Sparrow

Safflower:
Mourning Dove, Northern Cardinal, Song Sparrow, White-throated Sparrow, Purple Finch, Evening Grosbeak, Blue Jay, Ring-necked PheasantCanary Seed:
House Finch, House Sparrow, Mourning Dove, Purple Finch, Song Sparrow, White-crowned Sparrow, White-throated Sparrow, Dark-eyed Junco, Rosy Finch, Rufous-sided Towhee

Buckwheat:
Mourning Dove

Sunflower Seeds and Peanuts

Sunflower Seed:
American Goldfinch, Blue Jay, chickadees, Common Grackle, Evening Grosbeak, House Finch, House Sparrow, Mourning Dove, Northern Cardinal, Purple Finch, Song Sparrow, White-crowned Sparrow, White-throated Sparrow, Red-winged Blackbird, Rusty Blackbird, Mountain Chickadee, Boreal Chickadee, Red- and White-winged Crossbill, Cassin's Finch, Pine Grosbeak, Gray and Steller's Jay, magpies, Clark's Nutcracker, Red-breasted and White-breasted Nuthatch, Common and Hoary Redpoll, Pine Siskin, Downy and Hairy Woodpecker, Bobwhite and Gambel's Quail, Cedar Waxwing.

Peanuts:
Chickadees, Common Grackle, House Finch, Blue Jay, Scrub Jay, White-crowned Sparrow, White-throated Sparrow

Peanut Hearts:
Common Grackle, House Finch, Mourning Dove, Song Sparrow, White-crowned Sparrow, White-throated Sparrow

Seed should be stored in a cool dry area, well swept to keep mice and rats away. Green plastic garbage cans make excellent containers for storage, the large ones easily holding 25 to 50 kg of seed mix. It is important to keep the seeds dry. Since the aspergillus mold that grows on wet seed is toxic to birds, damp, mouldy seeds should be thrown out.

Suet and Peanut Butter

During the winter, foods with a high fat content are an important part of the diet of insectivorous birds like woodpeckers, magpies and creepers. In very cold weather carbohydrates cannot provide enough energy for birds to survive cold nights or snowstorms. Only fat provides enough energy. For this reason suet and peanut butter feeders are very popular with a number of birds, including some that aren't likely to come in for other foods, such as the Pileated Woodpecker. Even seed-eating birds prefer seeds with a high oil content; this may explain why rice is not a very popular food for northern birds in the winter, while sunflower seeds are.

Suet is the hard fat found around the kidneys and heart of cattle and sheep, but any beef or pork fat can be substituted for it. In fact, it is easier and definitely cheaper to get fat trimmings from the butcher than to pay for suet balls. The unprocessed, crumbly suet sold at the supermarket in small bags for mince pies and other cooking purposes makes a nice supplement to the fat trimmings, but because of the cost, it should be put out in a small hanging, swinging container so that magpies and Blue Jays don't eat it all before the other birds get some. Fat trimmings tend to become dehydrated when the temperatures are low, and must be replaced every three or four weeks (or whenever the birds seem to lose interest in them). While large pieces of pork fat, nailed to the trunk of a tree, can be used for food, bacon drippings are not good for the birds because of the large amounts of salt and nitrates added during processing. Traditionally, suet is put out only during the winter, but rendered fat doesn't spoil in the heat like unrendered fat does, and can be left out year round.

In addition to suet, peanut butter is also a good addition to a feeder's menu. In fact, peanut butter is often the secret ingredient for increasing bird activity.

Suet:

Screech Owl, Northern Flicker, American Crow, Red-bellied Woodpecker, Hairy Woodpecker, Downy Wood-pecker, Blue and Gray Jay, Clark's Nutcracker, Boreal Chickadee, Mountain Chickadee, Carolina Chickadee, Black-capped Chickadee, Tufted Titmouse, Bushtit, White-breasted Nuthatch, Red-breasted Nuthatch, Brown Creeper, Carolina Wren, Mockingbird, Catbird, Curve-billed Thrasher, American Robin, Hermit Thrush, Golden-crowned Kinglet, Ruby-crowned Kinglet, Northern Shrike, European Star-ling, Myrtle Warbler, Pine Warbler, Ovenbird, Red-winged Blackbird, Baltimore Oriole, grackles, Rose-breasted Gros-beak, juncos, Tree Sparrow, White-throated Sparrow, Pileated Woodpecker

Peanut Butter:

Northern Flicker, Hairy Woodpecker, Downy Woodpecker, Blue Jay, Steller's Jay, Black-capped Chickadee, Boreal Chickadee, Mountain Chickadee, Chestnut-backed Chicka-dee, White- and Red-breasted Nuthatch, Brown Creeper, Curve-billed Thrasher, American Robin, Varied Thrush, Oregon Brown Towhee, juncos, Tree Sparrow

More specialized mixtures of fat and other ingredients can be made to provide the birds with a little variety and additional protein. Since suet and peanut butter eaters do not usually eat a lot of different seeds, it is better to add good sources of protein to their mix rather than seeds. The mixtures begin with rendered fat which can be made by cutting up suet or fat, or putting it through a food processor. Melt it in small batches in the oven (120°C), microwave or frying pan and then use a colander or sieve lined with cheesecloth to strain out any meat, rind or impurities. This process can be repeated for a smoother fat if necessary.

Sweet Suet

Add sugar syrup (a boiled mixture of 1 part sugar to 4 parts water) to a mixture of suet, peanut butter, flour, and cornmeal. Form mixture into balls.

Peanut Butter and Suet

Mix peanut butter with hot, rendered suet. Let cool.

Year-round Mix

Mix together vegetable shortening, peanut butter, cornmeal and flour.

Cornballs

Mix one part peanut butter and one part rendered suet with six parts cornmeal. Form into balls or spoon into muffin papers and let cool. These can be made in large batches and kept in the freezer.

Jay Jubilee

This recipe uses suet or twice-melted fat; when fat is melted a second time, it sets harder when it cools and can better hold the mixture of seeds and nuts. (John Janzen Nature Centre)

60 mL meat scraps, ground
250 mL cracked corn
250 mL crushed peanuts
5 mL sand
250 mL twice-melted fat

Mix dry ingredients together and place in a dish or foil pan. Pour melted fat over them and refrigerate until firm.

Much more complicated combinations of foods are possible, served in hardened cakes, spooned into suet logs, or spread on pine cones. Typical concoctions may include chopped fruit (raisins, dates, figs, apples, berries, moist but not dry coconut), grains (bran, rolled oats, barley flakes, corn in almost any form, whole wheat flour, cream of wheat, wheat germ), protein (cottage cheese, dog food, pellets for rabbits or gerbils, cat food, grated or cubed cheese), miscellaneous goodies (popcorn, noodles, pastry, sand, crushed eggshells) and insects collected during the summer (ant eggs, mealworms, reconstituted freeze-dried larvae for tropical fish, tent caterpillars). The combinations are almost endless.

Ideas for Summer

Summer provides a new challenge in attracting birds to the back yard, since winter visitors will be joined by the returning migrants who often prefer different foods, especially insects, fruits and berries. Nesting birds also have different food needs, particularly in what they provide for their young. Almost all birds, even seed eaters, give their young a diet high in insects before they are fledged from the nest. This is because the young, rapidly growing birds need a lot of protein; once they have fledged, they are gradually introduced to their more normal diet. During this time, the parents also need a lot of food to keep up their own energy, so they are quick to use an easy source of appropriate food.

There are a number of foods that can be added to feeder in the summer to attract these birds, including a calcium supplement in late spring and early summer. Crossbills and Northern Finches need it after their limited winter diet, and egg-laying females of all species can use extra calcium. Possible sources of calcium include finely crushed oyster or clam shells, available at pet stores that carry tropical bird supplies.

A number of summer and migrating birds are as fond of sunflower seeds as winter birds, so be sure to keep some out for them. Put out some fruits and insects as well. Insects are perhaps the most difficult food to find, but pet and bait stores carry mealworms, and some tropical birds' pet stores have special mixes for insectivores.

If Baltimore Orioles are in the neighbourhood, they can be brought into the back yard with sliced oranges. Attach the orange round to a tree trunk or post with a nail. Make sure there's a convenient perch near the orange.

A good mix of foods for summer can include the following: chopped suet; peanut butter (mixed with cornmeal); a standard seed mixture; oatmeal or rice with raisins; walnuts (chopped or in the half-shell); crushed filberts, pecans or hazelnuts; fruits (cut apples, raisins, cherries, bananas, oranges, pears, plums, peaches, dates, figs, wild berries); and wet, dry or canned pet food. Coconut shells or grapefruit halves are excellent serving cups for a fruit mixture, which can be made up in large quantities and frozen in small batches. Birds also enjoy fresh coconut meat.

Hummingbirds

This is also the time of year to add a hummingbird feeder. Even if you've never seen a hummingbird in your neighbourhood, you may attract one; if not, grosbeaks, tanagers, and some warblers will still use the feeders, as will House Sparrows and finches. Only a sugar water or commercial mix should be used, since honey may contain a fungus that is toxic to hummingbirds. For a home made solution, begin with a mix of 1 part sugar to 4 parts water. Most commercially produced feeders already have red on them, so the food doesn't need to be coloured at all. Hummingbird feeders are best placed near potted plants or by a flowering, hanging basket. A red construction-paper flower can be attached to the base of the feeding tube as a substitute. Once the hummingbird has found the feeder, the paper flower can be discarded. After the birds have started to come, the sugar concentration should be reduced to 1 to 6 parts or 1 to 9 parts. Too much of a highly concentrated solution can lead to liver damage, but too weak a concentration won't provide enough energy to make the stop worthwhile.

If the feeder is hung near a good perch, hummingbirds will spend more time in the yard, resting on the perch between feedings. One of the difficulties of attracting hummingbirds, however, is that they can become very territorial about their feeders. One bird can decide that the feeder belongs to him, and he'll spend most of the summer chasing others away from it. On the other hand some feeders are used comfortably by ten to fifteen different birds with very little squabbling. If one possessive bird is becoming a problem, try hanging a second feeder around the corner or at the opposite side of the house from the first one. With luck you'll have a host of chattering, iridescent hummingbirds to keep you company on summer evenings.

Other Foods

Sparrows and Rock Doves aren't the only birds who like "human" food. Pastry and baked goods are popular with a number of species. Magpies and Blue Jays will eat just about anything, from stale cake to left-over spaghetti, and robins are partial to ground-up toast. Some other foods that have tempted the palate of individual species are: corn bread, cottage cheese, bran muffins, and fried potatoes. It's important to remember, though, that in cold, northern winters, white bread isn't nutritious enough to keep the birds alive. It's best to avoid it altogether. Watermelon, pumpkin, squash and cantaloupe seeds don't have to go to waste; just wash and dry them and put them out for the birds.

Unshelled nuts are another popular treat. Walnuts are particularly popular with Blue Jays, chickadees, titmice, nuthatches, Brown Thrashers, Myrtle Warblers, cardinals, juncos, House Finches and White-crowned and Song Sparrows. But don't stop at walnuts. Try hazelnuts, almonds, pecans, Brazil nuts, or whatever else is available. Just crack the shells open and let the birds pick out the meat for themselves. Put out only unsalted nuts, as too much salt is harmful to the birds.

Another treat for magpies, woodpeckers and Brown Creepers is bone paste, the mixture of marrow, fat and bone powder that is created when a butcher saws through meat bones. It spoils very quickly in warm weather (above freezing), so it's really only a winter food. Spread some up the side of a tree for the Brown Creepers and woodpeckers. Magpies also like it, and bone paste can be rolled into balls and frozen for future use.

Feel free to try a wide variety of foods to supplement the basic seed mix and sunflower seeds. But remember that it's important to have a busy yard to attract unusual birds. They may only pass through during migration or, if resident, may have a large territory to move around in, and they won't be attracted to a silent, empty yard. So don't begrudge the House Sparrows, Blue Jays and magpies their food. They're the PR men for back yards, spreading the news about the best place to eat in the neighbourhood.

Grit

Grit is an important ingredient in birds' diets. They have to keep some in their crop to help grind up the seeds they eat before they can digest them. This is an easy item to include at the feeders. Either buy the packages of grit that are sold for pet birds or use beach sand or crushed charcoal. It can be put out separately, in a container or scattered on a sidewalk or driveway, or it can be added to their seed mixture, approximately one handful per gallon of seed.

Adding Water

A lot of neighbourhood birds, such as Vireos, tanagers and Ovenbirds will never come to a bird feeder. But they will come to a bird bath, especially if there is the sound of splashing water to attract them.

Garden, hardware and lawn ornament stores often have several varieties of bird baths, or they can be made from almost any type of container. Just be sure that the water is no deeper than 6 cm at any point in the bowl and that the birds have a perch around the edge or a landing platform in the centre. They also need a perch nearby where they can sit and preen themselves after bathing; a branch, wire or fence

will do. Some materials that can be used to make a birdbath include garbage can lids, trays from ceramic pots, aluminum pie pans, and flagstones with a natural depression. Be sure to flush out birdbaths frequently and clean out any built-up algae and scum.

The sound of dripping or moving water will attract birds much more quickly than a container of still water; however, it's not necessary to spend hundreds of dollars on a circulating pump and multilevel fountains. The simplest solution is to suspend a bucket or container with a small hole in the bottom over the birdbath. A fast, steady drip is enough to attract birds. You can also check with hardware or garden stores for commercially made devices that work off a garden hose.

A small container of water can be provided on a shelf feeder, and a small birdbath will fit on a balcony. Suspending a plastic container with a small hole above it will create a drip effect.

During the winter birds get water by eating snow, but they will quickly take advantage of a source of open water. Birdbaths with built-in heaters are available. Check with a local nature centre or garden centre to see if they know of a source, or order one through American bird magazines or catalogues. When making a heated birdbath at home, it is very important to make sure that the system doesn't electro-cute the birds. Systems using a metal or ceramic dish suspended over a 25- or 50- watt light bulb are common, as well as those with an immersion water heater designed for a depth of 2 to 8 cm.

If there is no space for such an intricate birdbath, birds can still benefit from a small container filled with hot water from a kettle. The birds use the birdbath as a hot tub as much as a drinking source. Apparently they enjoy standing in the hot water just to feel warmer for a while.

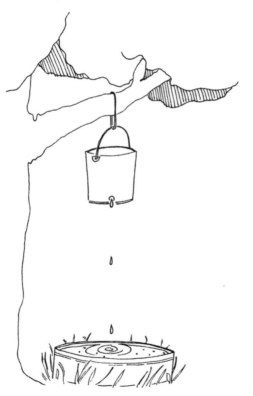

A bucket hanging over the birdbath can provide the sound of dripping water which quickly attracts birds in the summer. If the birds don't respond, try to increase the speed of the drip.

When To Put Out Food

Winter

Winter is the most common time for putting out food for the birds, since natural foods are scarcer then and can be harder to find under the snow. Winter bird residents appreciate an easy source of food, especially during cold spells and after a snowstorm. Activity at a feeder often triples after a snowfall, particularly the first one of the winter, so it's important to make sure that your feeders are full. It may be necessary to brush the snow off table or shelf feeders so the birds can get to the food more easily.

In winter, birds which are hard to find at other times of the year or that nest far north in the boreal forest, like Pine Grosbeaks, siskins, redpolls, Evening Grosbeaks and Bohemian Waxwings, may be frequent visitors to the feeders.

Summer

Many people stop feeding the birds at the end of winter, thinking that the availability of natural food will make birds less interested in coming to their feeders, and that putting food out for them will be a waste of money. But during the summer a new set of birds can be attracted that aren't around during the winter. This is a good time to see Rose-breasted Grosbeaks, House Wrens, Chipping Sparrows, Baltimore Orioles, Tree Swallows, Purple Martins, and a number of other small nesters. Nesting birds also need a lot of food while they are raising their young, and a well stocked feeder can help provide it for them.

Spring and Fall

Keeping out food for the birds is also important during the spring. If there's a sudden spring snowstorm, that food supply will become critical, especially for the migrants returning from the south. Spring and fall are also good times of the year to see migratory birds passing through the neighbourhood. Many of these special birds tend to be ground feeders, so it's a good idea to keep some seed and cracked corn spread on the ground under a spruce or some shrubbery. The feeding activity of local residents, particularly House Sparrows, will tell the migrants where the ground food is. New birds which may be attracted at this time of year include Harris' Sparrows, Fox Sparrows, Lincoln's Sparrows, and White-throated Sparrows.

Having food out during the fall also helps establish the yard as a regular feeding stop for the birds that will reside in the area during the winter. When the first snowfall hits, they'll know exactly where to go, and they won't be lost to feeding stations on other streets or yards.

Other Amenities For The Yard

Nesting Boxes

Birds fiercely compete for nesting areas. While most birds find adequate nesting space in tree limbs, cavity nesters are having a harder time in most cities. Rather than constructing a nest on a tree branch, these birds build nests inside cavities of old trees, posts or buildings. Since woodlots and forests are becoming increasingly rare in Canadian cities, and since most homeowners remove dead wood, good nesting spots are becoming harder to find. House Sparrows add to the problem, since they nest earlier in the spring than

native birds and often take the best nesting spots. That means fewer young birds of native species can be produced each year, and the numbers of cavity-nesting wild birds decrease. The problem can be alleviated by putting out nesting boxes in the yard. Although keeping the House Sparrows and European Starlings out can be a challenge, it can be done with diligence, and careful selection and maintenance of your birdhouses.

While birds work very hard to establish a territory and to keep out members of their own species, they don't pay much attention to other species. Thus it is possible to have several different species — pairs of robins, chickadees, wrens, orioles and hummingbirds, for example — all nesting in one backyard. On the other hand, sparrows can be very destructive to nesting birds, particularly if they want a certain nesting site. There are two techniques that can be used to help desirable species establish successful nests in the back yard. First, make sure that the nesting boxes put out for them are the proper shape with the right size of entrance hole. For smaller birds, like chickadees and wrens, keep the entrance hole less than 3 cm (1 1/4 inches) in diameter so that sparrows can't fit through. If the bird house is made of wood, add a small metal ring or some smooth sheet metal around the entrance to keep squirrels and sparrows from enlarging the hole. Secondly, keep the entrance holes to houses for larger birds blocked up until the sparrows have established their own nest sites. In the fall take the bird-house down, or block its hole to keep sparrows, mice or squirrels from roosting there for the winter.

The location and landscaping of a yard are important determining factors for what birds will be attracted to the nest boxes. There's no sense in putting up boxes for blue-birds or martins in the city or the suburbs. Bluebirds like to nest on fence posts along open country fields, and Purple Martins like an open yard near a lake or large pond. On the other hand, a yard with trees will attract chickadees, wrens, flickers, Tree Swallows, and nuthatches.

Nature centres and hardware stores have birdhouses for sale. Be sure that the entrance hole is the right size, and that the house has ventilation holes at the bottom. Check with the nature centre or library for plans for more specialized nesting boxes to build yourself.

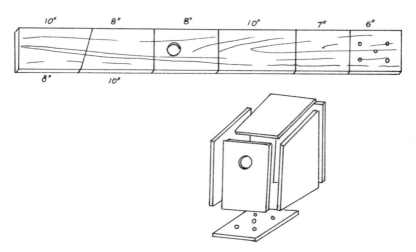

Birdhouses should be put at least 2 m off the ground, in a location shaded from the sun; nuthatches prefer their nesting boxes at least 3 to 8 m above the ground. Be sure the boxes are level or tilted downwards so that the entrance is sheltered from rain and wind. The outside can be painted a light colour to keep the houses cooler, but the inside should not be painted. Use natural wood 2 to 2.5 cm thick. Cedar, plywood or redwood that has not been treated with chemical preservatives works best.

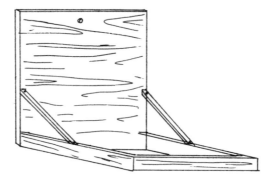

Nesting shelves can attract American Robins, phoebes, or Barn Swallows. Place them on a wall up under the eave in a protected area since crows, magpies, and Blue Jays have been known to eat the eggs and young of bracket nesters.

The birdhouse should have a side that opens, so that the old nest can be cleaned out in the fall or spring. After removing the old material spray the inside with creolin (1 part creolin to 10 parts water) to kill bird lice and other insects.

Nesting Material

Whether or not you have birdhouses, you can still provide nesting materials for the birds. Use a plastic fruit basket and fill it with long grasses, string, yarn or white duck feathers. String can also be draped over branches or put in an onion bag. Make sure the pieces of string are no more than 15 to 20 cm long. Birds have been known to become tangled in large loops of string woven into their nests and hang themselves.

If swallows, Wood Thrushes or phoebes are in the area, they can be provided with some mud for their nests. Fill a shallow cake pan with clay and garden soil and add water until it becomes nice and muddy, with a consistency of modelling clay.

Roosting Boxes

Cold nights and winter storms are critical periods for birds in the winter. To survive them they need, in addition to the proper foods, a good sheltered spot to roost in. Spruces, evergreens, openings in buildings and old birdhouses are some of the most popular spots. But roosting boxes that will provide birds with a warm, protected place can be built. Several birds of different species can use such a box. The combined effect of their body heat will keep them warmer than if they all roosted separately.

If building a roosting box is impractical, leave a birdhouse open during the winter so birds can roost at night; open birdhouses could be occupied by unwanted sparrows and squirrels, however.

 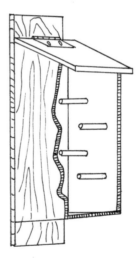

Dimensions: 25 cm square, 1 m high, 8 cm entrance hole only 5 cm above floor (lets the heat rise to the top of the box), staggered perches (so birds are not sitting directly above or below another bird). Hang the box 2 to 3 m above the ground with the entrance facing south.

Dust Bath

Birds like to take a dust bath in order to keep mites and other insects under control. They can be provided with such a spot by putting a mixture of one part each, sand, loam and ashes in a small corner of the yard.

Brush Pile

A brush pile will provide the birds with a little extra cover and a safe area to hide whenever hawks or cats come around. Begin with some large tree limbs or branches of shrubs which can be crisscrossed on top of one another, then add some lighter limbs to the pile. Cover the pile with small evergreen branches for cover from rain and snow. If a cut tree is left over from Christmas, it can be added as well. If the pile is dismantled during spring cleanup, save the large limbs for next year's pile.

Landscaping For Birds

Back yard plants play an important role in creating an attractive environment for birds in three ways: they provide food, shelter from the cold and snow, and nesting places. The layout and type of plants help determine what birds will be attracted. A heavily treed yard attracts forest birds like nuthatches, Brown Creepers, thrushes and tanagers. An open yard with some shrubs will be attractive to birds of the open country like quail, American Goldfinches and Tree Sparrows.

Designing or redesigning a yard to improve its attractiveness to birds need not be difficult. A professional landscape architect can help (a service often provided free by lawn and garden stores), or one can do it alone.

The important thing to remember about landscaping for birds and other wildlife is that they can't use a neat, overly groomed yard. They prefer a "wild" yard because it provides them with the resources they need— food from seeds, fruits and insect-rich old wood; nesting spots in shrub and tree cover; and winter roosting areas in evergreens. A beautifully cut and edged lawn with open, weeded flowerbeds isn't going to have many birds in it. However, a yard doesn't have to go to ruin in order to attract birds. The goal is to provide a mix of as many habitats and foods as possible, to attract the widest variety of birds. By choosing appropriate trees, shrubs, vines and flowers, the birds can have those elements of a wild environment that they need, and the homeowner can still have a beautiful, socially acceptable yard.

In planning a yard for birds, there needs to be a balance between the open lawn and the forest-like canopy of trees. A combination of open and treed spaces produces a transition

Four vegetation heights utilized by birds—from left to right: trees, low trees or high shrubs, low shrubs and open grass.

area, called the edge, that provides more food and cover than either environment alone. The increase in wildlife activity in an area that has been opened up within a forest, or in an area of trees and cover that has been added to an open space is called the "edge effect." This becomes a good place to put feeders, since more birds will be naturally attracted to that area. Several height levels can also add variety to the birds' environment; high trees, low trees, shrubs, ground cover and open lawn all make a yard more attractive to both birds and humans. A rock wall or vine-covered wall or trellis will also add height changes that are attractive to birds.

An open yard with a feeding and water area in the centre.

For an open yard, some shrubs should be added around the edges or in a central island to give the birds cover. This then becomes a good place to put a feeder and birdbath. A fruiting tree will provide perches for birds as they enter the yard. If the neighbourhood is heavily treed, the yard will provide an edge within the "forest" and will offer an oasis of openness for birds that prefer those areas or that use both the forest and the open.

For a yard with heavier planting, use a mix of deciduous and evergreen trees. Evergreens are particularly important for providing cover during the winter. A good mix between open and treed areas will yield the greatest variety of birds, but it is also important to remember that treed areas also need shrubs. Many yards are planted with either a ring of shrubs or of trees. Shrubs provide good nesting areas, cover and food, but a mix of shrubs, ground cover and trees gives you a very rich forest effect which will attract a number of birds, improving over the years as it develops and matures. With this type of habitat, one can attract birds which will not come to a feeder but will find their own food in the leaf litter or bare ground in your "forest," such as Ovenbirds, Northern Waterthrushes, and Fox Sparrows. Fallen leaves can also be left under the trees to give birds like thrushes, Ovenbirds, and White-crowned and White-throated Sparrows a good area for feeding on insects.

A fully landscaped yard with mature trees to provide cover and nesting areas.

TREES

Alder	Flowering dogwood	Oak
Ash	Hackberry	Persimmon
Beech	Hawthorn	Pine
Birch	Helmock	Poplar
Cherry	Maple	Red cedar
Crab apple	Mountain ash	Spruce
Elm	Mulberry	

SHRUBS

Barberry
Bittersweet
Blackberry
Elderberry
Firethorn
Gooseberry
High bush cranberry

Juniper
Nanking Cherry
Raspberry
Rhododendro
Rose
Saskatoon
Silver buffaloberry

Snowberry
Viburnum
Wayfaring Tree

FLOWERING PLANTS

Amaranthus
Asters
Bachelor's buttons
Black-eyed susans
Calendula
California poppies
Campanula
Carduus
Chrysanhemums
Columbines

Coreopsis
Cosmos
Dianthus
English violet
Forget-me-nots
Four-o-clocks
Gallardias
Larkspurs
Love-in-a-mist
Marigolds

Petunias
Phlox
Portulaca
Scabiosa
Showy stonecrop
Statice
Strawberries
Sunflowers
Verbena
Zinnias

DECORATIVE GRASSES

Quaking grass
Love grass
Hare's tail grass
Crimson fountain grass
Plains bristle grass

FLOWERS TO ATTRACT HUMMINGBIRDS

Annuals
Four-o'clock
Fuchsia
Impatiens
Maltese Cross
Morning
Glory
Nasturtuim
Nicotiana
Pentstemon
Petunia
Scarlet runner bean
Zinnia

Perennials
Bee Balm
Bugleweed
Butterfly milkweed
Coral bells
Dahlia
Dephinium
Evening primrose
False dragonhead
Gladiola
Hollyhock
Lythrum
Phystotegia
Periwinkle
Sage
Tiger lily
Verbena
Weigela
Yucca

Solving Problems

Squirrels

Most books on feeding birds imply that it is necessary to wage war upon all the squirrels in the neighbourhood. Often there is the assumption that squirrels eating at your feeders are undesirable, or that a yard will be overrun by them. Therefore a number of squirrel baffles are usually suggested, as well as ways to position feeders in order to make them inaccessible to squirrels. However, squirrels are intelligent and persistent, and if they want to reach a particular feeder, they probably will learn how either to master the baffle or to get around it.

So don't try to keep a squirrel-free yard. Just try to keep them controlled so that they don't keep the birds away from the feeders. Birds are used to dealing with squirrels, as they are with dominant birds, and will keep an eye on them while feeding or will wait for them to finish before coming in to a feeder. Anti-squirrel devices can be used to keep a few feeders free for birds. This will be particularly effective if food is also provided for the squirrels in a separate location. Don't start a war unless the yard is overwhelmed with squirrels. Red squirrels tend to be very territorial and don't easily share feeders, so gangs of them won't dominate the feeders. Grey squirrels, on the other hand, are more sociable. They are also less nervous than red squirrels and can feed comfortably with birds, particularly on the ground. Don't worry about a problem before it occurs; besides, the squirrels can be just as enjoyable as the birds.

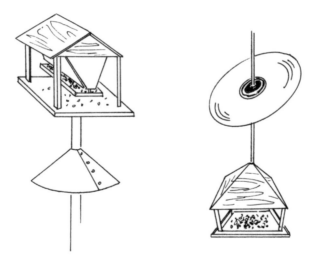

Two types of baffles to keep squirrels out of the feeder. Right: *metal cone to keep squirrels from climbing up the pole.* Left: *a 33 1/2 rpm record to keep squirrels from climbing down the wire.*

Cats

Controlling cats can be a more difficult problem. Try to position the feeders so that the birds cannot be easily ambushed, and put up wire fences to slow the cats down. If magpies or Blue Jays start to make a loud racket, they have probably found a cat. Go out and help them chase it away. If a cat is in the yard lying in wait for the birds, spray it with the garden hose. If it gets chased away, it won't come back as often. If a neighbour's cat is a particular problem, you can ask them to put a bell on it so that the birds will at least have some warning. Perhaps the best solution is to get a dog. Encourage the dog to chase cats out of the yard, but don't let it hurt them.

Dominant Birds

It's natural for birds to have a pecking order at the feeders. Larger or more aggressive birds often chase away others while they are eating. Fighting for position at the feeder happens all the time when any large flock arrives. By providing several feeders with room for birds on both sides, some of the pressure can be alleviated and more birds will be able to feed with less squabbling.

Window Kills

Every year many birds are killed by flying into windows. When attracting birds, it is likely that some will fly into the windows and be injured or killed. This problem can be minimized with some simple remedies. Birds tend to fly into windows because they see a strong reflection of the trees, lawn and sky and think they're just flying into another area of the yard. The most dangerous windows are those that are aligned with another window so that the bird can see clearly through the house. The misleading reflection can be broken up and the window made visible to the birds by putting an obstruction between the two windows, moving feeders away from the problem windows, or hanging wind chimes, a mobile, or some other distracting object in front of the window. Most nature centres also sell hawk silhouettes that you put on the window, on the theory that the birds will think a hawk is flying around in that area and avoid it. On the other hand, perhaps the silhouettes just let the birds see the window in the same sense that decals or decorations on a sliding glass door show when it is closed. Decorative decals could be put on the window or stained glass decorations hung in it to break up the reflection and better define the glass area.

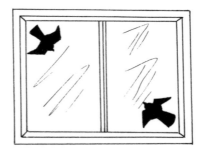

The biggest problem with window crashes comes in the spring and fall when migrants are moving through. Residents of the yard tend to know the area very well and don't seem to make the same mistake about windows that migrants or other strangers do.

If a bird does crash into the window and is stunned but not dead, it can be brought inside and left to rest in a dark box in a warm quiet place. According to the Calgary Zoo, the bird's disorientation and dizziness is caused by the collection of blood in the brain resulting from the blow against the window. If the bird is given a couple of drops of a mixture of 1 part water to 1 part brandy, it will increase circulation and speed up the reabsorption of the blood. When it has recovered, release it in some shrubbery so it has a protected place to rest and reorient itself before taking off.

Reflection Battles

One other problem with windows, not as widely recognized, is that of male birds fighting their reflections, thinking they are chasing off a challenger for their territory. This can be very harmful to a nesting pair, since a male can expend a lot of time and energy on this fruitless battle when he should be building a nest or providing food for his young. He may also be driven away from the territory when he finds himself unable to chase away his ghostly opponent. This can be stopped by finding some way to eliminate the reflection. Try putting a fine mesh screen over the window; a flat white, light-coloured, or patterned board (or paper) inside the window, right up against the glass; or cover up the window from the outside.

Myths about feeding birds

Once you start putting out food in the winter, you have to continue until spring or the birds will starve.

This is a very common myth. Birds have a large feeding range (which varies from species to species), and they are used to food supplies that come and go from season to season. It is natural for them to exploit a food source while it exists, and to find something else when it is gone. Feeder stations are usually just one stop on a bird's daily rounds, so they will not starve if food can't be put out regularly. If the supply of food is only sporadic not as many birds will visit the yard, but putting up a feeder for a weekend at a campground or for several weeks at a cabin won't hurt anything and will provide enjoyable entertainment.

You can't use metal in your feeders because birds' eyes and feet will freeze to it.

Bare metal is probably not the most comfortable perch for birds in the winter but it won't hurt them. Their feet are dry and scaly and don't freeze to metal, and birds are agile and quick enough that they don't let their eyes come into contact with the cold metal of a suet container. However, that doesn't mean they don't *prefer* wooden perches to metal ones.

Birds will choke to death on plain peanut butter so you must add cornmeal or suet to it.

Some birds have been found dead with peanut butter in their mouths, but it is not clear that this was the actual cause of death. They may have been killed by flying into a window when startled at the peanut butter feeder, or they may have been quite ill and died before they could finish their meal. One can play it safe and add something to the peanut butter in very warm weather, but don't be too concerned.

Conclusion

I've mentioned the names of a lot of different birds in this book. Some of them will be found in your area, and some won't. Many of them you may not recognize. You don't need to know the names of the different species to be able to enjoy seeing them; however, it can add to your appreciation. You can find a number of bird guides that will help you identify the species coming to your yard, either using a complete guide for all Canada or a local guide for your city or province. In addition to identification, the guide should tell you a little about the bird, where it spends the winter and where it nests, the type of habitat it likes and perhaps even the type of food it prefers.

You may also want to get a pair of binoculars to help you get a closer look at birds at their feeders and in other parts of the yard or trees. Camera departments or stores carry them in a variety of prices and sizes. You can check your library for birding publications that will help you understand the different styles and choose the one best suited for your use.

You may also want to start a yard list, which is exactly what it says— a list of all the different species that have been in your yard at least once. We also like to keep track of the date when we see the first of a species at the feeders or in the yard each year, and, if it is a migrant, how long it stays around.

If you wish, you can keep your new hobby at the level of putting out food in your yard, or you can become much more involved with birding.

If you enjoy photography, you can try photographing birds— at the feeder, the birdbath, or their nests. Birds can be very challenging subjects.

Through nature centres, book stores or specialty mail order catalogues, you can get record albums, cassettes or CDs that will teach you the songs of the different species of birds. By learning to recognize a bird's song, you can learn what species are around you even when you can't see them. During the summer you often know a lot more about birds in the neighbourhood by what you hear than by what you see.

Most cities have a bird club or Audubon society that will welcome your membership. They often organize field trips to good birding areas, and are willing to help beginners improve their skills in bird identification.

If you want to become a full-fledged birder, you can take your hobby with you wherever you travel. With the appropriate bird guide and a pair of binoculars you can enjoy birds all around the world. There are a number of interesting places that are noted for their birds, even in your own province. Check the bookstores and nature centres for a local wildlife viewing guide. Some of the special places that birders from all over the world like to go are: Point Pelee

National Park, Ontario, during the spring migration of birds; Beaverhill Lake, Alberta, for summer waterfowl; Everglades National Park, Florida, for subtropical birds; the Galapagos Islands, Ecuador, for their unique birds and wildlife; Costa Rica for tropical birds; Madera Canyon, Arizona, for hummingbirds. Check your local library and bookstore for books about nature and birding, and ask about magazines written just for birders.

Every year at Christmas the Cornell School of Ornithology sponsors the Christmas Bird Count. All across North America, communities organize local participation in the count, the aim of which is to record every bird seen on that one day so that the records can be compared from year to year. You can volunteer as a participant, whether as a bush beater (one who goes out around the neighbourhoods or through the fields to count the birds they find) or as a feeder watcher (one who provides a count of the birds that have come to their feeder on that day). Contact your local nature centre, bird club or Audubon society for information.

I hope you'll take this information and create an enjoyable and successful yard full of birds and wildlife. For more information about birding and feeding birds check with your library, bookstore and nature centre. Don't be afraid to experiment, and don't be discouraged if there are lulls in feeding activity. There are often new surprises just ahead, and old friends to welcome back from their winter migrations.

YARD LIFE LIST

Species   Notes

_____   _____

_____   _____

_____   _____

_____   _____

_____   _____

_____   _____

_____   _____

_____   _____

_____   _____

_____   _____

_____   _____

_____   _____

_____   _____

_____   _____

_____   _____

_____   _____

Species   Notes

BIRD LIFE LIST

*A list of the all the species of Birds that I have
seen at least once*

Species	Date	Notes

Species	Date	Notes
_____	_____	_____
_____	_____	_____
_____	_____	_____
_____	_____	_____
_____	_____	_____
_____	_____	_____
_____	_____	_____
_____	_____	_____
_____	_____	_____
_____	_____	_____
_____	_____	_____
_____	_____	_____
_____	_____	_____
_____	_____	_____
_____	_____	_____
_____	_____	_____
_____	_____	_____
_____	_____	_____
_____	_____	_____

Species	Date	Notes

PARTS OF A BIRD

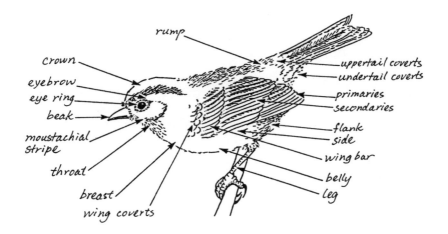

LONE PINE BIRD BOOKS

Birds of Edmonton (revised) — Robin Bovey
ISBN 0-919433-80-4   128pp   5 1/2 x 8 1/2 $9.95

Birds of Calgary (revised) — Robin Bovey
ISBN 0-919433-82-0   128pp   5 1/2 x 8 1/2 $9.95

Birds of Victoria — Bovey, Campbell, Gates
ISBN 0-919433-75-8   144pp   5 1/2 x 8 1/2 $11.95

Birds of Vancouver — Robin Bovey & Wayne Campbell
ISBN 0-919433-73-1   144pp   5 1/2 x 8 1/2 $11.95

Birds of Toronto — Gerald McKeating
ISBN 0-919433-63-4   144pp   5 1/2 x 8 1/2 $9.95

Birds of Ottawa — Gerald McKeating
ISBN 0-919433-64-2   144pp   5 1/2 x 8 1/2 $9.95

Birdwatching is quickly becoming one of the most popular pastimes in the world, and is one which may be practised as easily in one's own back yard as in the wilderness.

These guides identify the birds most likely to be seen in the back yard, in streets, in parks and in natural areas of Canada's major cities.

Each book is filled with advice on feeding birds, building and siting nesting boxes for birds, as well as a section on making your own garden more attractive for birds.

Written by local bird experts and beautifully illustrated throughout, these full-colour books are easy-to-use and indispensable references to the birds of your community.

Watch for *Birds of Winnipeg* and *Birds of Halifax* to be released in Spring, 1992.

Buy these and other Lone Pine books from your local bookstore or order directly through Lone Pine Publishing, #206, 10426 - 81 Avenue, Edmonton, Alberta, T6E 1X5.

Prices shown do not include GST.